to the humans who broke us. to everything that made us who we are today.

may our love shine on.

-z.k.d

Made By The Broken

Poetry & Prose

By: Zachry K. Douglas

i always seem to give more to the one i am with
than they give back to me. i am sure it is some
god-awful curse some souls are born to carry.
it isn't as frustrating as it has been before,
but it still hurts all the same. it makes me
wonder if i will ever find someone who will
allow themselves to be more than who they are.
i did not choose this. it was given to me long before
i had a heartbeat. long before my skin could reflect
light. long before my tongue was chewed off by my
own teeth that once sharpened the bones of my
enemy. love is not a war you should have to fight
alone. maybe one day, someone can come into
my life ready for what i am and be thankful for
it. until then, i will maintain my existence and
love every fucking thing that touches my face,
as if it were a sleeping ocean made of infinite
waves, crashing wildly against all of those who
have tried to battle me for what i have, instead
of simply asking for it.

i know i am damaged property in the eyes of some.
i wear these scars on my arms knowing i have been
living in hell for quite some time, but not anymore.
i know it might be the first thing you see when
looking at me. i also know it is a story i will tell to
those who are willing to reveal their scars to me.
it's not a show and tell, just a soul's confession
you need to hear if you think you could be in my
life. i know i am far from what many would call,
"having it all figured out." i am as crazy and mad
as it gets, but in the most loving form. i know there
are probably better options for some than having
to help me carry my bags around, but i will never
let you wear that burden. life is an option and we
get hundreds of ways to go about living during the
day. when i look at my life, i know i have given
myself to each minute of what i have done. i am
a protector of those whom i love and an empath
when it comes to vibrating energies around me.
i collect them like people collect souvenirs. i have
always been more from of another world than
anywhere i have lived. in order to know someone,
you have to know where they have been, so the
story goes. i know what it feels like when people
don't believe you. it's hard for others to understand
anything else, when all they can tell you is that the
sky is blue and the grass is green.

i looked into your eyes and never saw you
as a way out of my own hell. i never wanted
anyone else to have to travel it besides me.
but here you are, being what has kept me in a
place where the light is safe and love remains.

being comfortable in our silence gives me
the ability to love you in ways i never could
give myself. you have made the quiet become
healing, when before, it had been what was
ripping me apart. my head falls onto the
pillow next to you, and the nightmares
finally have a place to forget what they
have seen and who had created them.

it's beautiful because it happened. that it transformed who i was. life is this way for certain people. you fight and fight and fight, then you are something, someone entirely different. nothing is more potent than change. nothing is more rewarding than being alive to have little moments that carve out the best of who you are. all the while saving the worst as a reminder to how we are all human. the little moments construct the universe in a way for us to visually and emotionally get through it all, somehow, some way. they are a spectacular confirmation of survival.

early this morning, after walking with the dawn,
we laid down in a patch of forgotten field outside
of town. we looked up and promised each other
we would always have this spot amongst the gods,
humans, and togetherness, within each
ray of light.

her laughter saved me from it all. not everyone
can make sense out of the space separating
themselves from reality, but what she gives me,
is something beyond a face i can recognize. it is
a cosmic sensation the universe feels right before
a star is born. her sincere adoration for anything
no one else dares to believe in is what keeps me
alive and believing in something more than
fate keeping us aligned.

i need you more than you know. you are the blood to my humanity. you are the life to my body. you are the eyes to my future. you are the hallelujah to my tomorrow. you are the destination to any home one would ever need. you are the constant beyond perfection. you are the skin on the trees and the rain that always falls for me. i need you more than you know. you are the adoration between the heart and soul. you are the wild keeping me safe. you are irreplaceable just as the moon is. i need you to be you, with me.

there you will always be, in all the places i
go and people i see. there you will always
be, in the heart of the sea and eyes of the
mountains looking down upon me.
there you will always be, kissing flowers
and counting stars. there you will always
be, walking amongst the crowd and
holding my hand so i don't get lost.
there you will always be, saying
goodnight to my soul and keeping
my love safe. as the darkness takes its
turn to replace the sun, there you will
always be, just for me.

the fear we keep can only hold us hostage if we
allow it to grab us by the throat and choke out
our truth. i am not human and have a difficult
time understanding the eyes of those who do
not see what i see. i am learning how to feel
everything around me without it taking my
own energy. i do not fear the darkness. i do
not fear the solitude. i am caught in-between
this world and the next. when i think about
this life, even angels love to burn.

do you love me or are you simply lonely?
space makes us incredibly longing for what
we need, even when love is whittled by our
own bones. my life misses the breaths you
once took alongside me. now, when i
breathe, it is for you and your absence.

my biggest fear is dying where i do not belong,
doing something i am not in love with. fear is
a funny thing, because without it, we would
never truly know what to go after. i wish to live
spontaneously with my eyes making love to every
adventure caught in their dreams. i am not from
here. i realize this more as each day passes,
i continue growing out of my flesh. i was born
with a thousand memories already living within me.
being a traveler, you must remain on your feet even
after you have fallen for the beauty around you. it is
the only way to know if you are still alive or chasing
ghosts leading you to an unmarked grave.

nothing feels better than knowing you are living
your best life. give yourself the love, commitment,
and relationship that will provide you with it all.
if you find yourself being the best option for those
things at this time, live it beautifully and regret free.
sometimes, we are who we need when everything
you feel, feels like a dead end road. once you
locate the beginning, the finality ceases to scare
away the possibilities you may never discover
if you continue to fear loneliness as meaning
being without someone else. being absent from
your own life is an open invitation for others
to leave you just the same.

i am tired of dying; my grave is full. i have been alive for nine years. i have died before and my mind was the murderer. for too long, i allowed it to ruin who i was and take advantage of my personal journey. i had a failed suicide attempt in May of 2009. i have my scars to look at each day to know i am alive for a reason. i took any pill i could find. i drank an entire bottle of Jose Cuervo. i ran the water in the tub and got in. the rest i will save due to the graphic nature of it. my grave has many versions of who i was and who i have been. i grew tired of living scared and full of anxiety. i grew tired of it all and decided to take control of my life. October 22nd will be my fifth year of sobriety. my life changed that night when i made the choice to leave the drink behind for good and began focusing on my life. it still isn't easy and i have my bad days, but i don't have a bad life. i know the hell i have been through and i am a better man, human, son, brother, and friend, because i knew if i didn't change, i wouldn't have made it much longer afterwards. to all of those who are struggling, you are not alone. you never will be. reach out to me if you feel compelled to. even if you don't, i plead to you to find someone to talk about it with. i love you and if you are hurting, i am sorry. it gets better though. if my life can, yours surely will. i promise you.

you cannot take away pain by inflicting more of it. you hurt, because you are afraid of something that may never come. you are suffering for no other reason than it feels better than to feel nothing at all. you will get through it, because you always do. one day, you will understand you don't have to endure it. one day, you will breathe in happiness and there won't be the taste of regret on any word said. i see you looking around as if it won't ever come. i see you wondering if you were born already carving out your next twenty years of misery. i see you sitting alone as often as you can to avoid others based off of their energy. i sympathize with you, because i hurt myself for so long over others who in the end, never gave a fuck about what i was going through. i need you to know it will get better. this storm is only here to clear out your path. it is not meant to destroy who you are. take on the challenge and you will learn how to find peace, instead of pieces of what could have been. i see you, all of you. every single day you hate it a little more and the further away you get from ever being someone who can love you, for you.

the beautiful nature of how it began made life easier.
it made life believable. it made us hopeful to keep
trying for an ending we never wanted to come.
life is more than just the days, months, and years.
it is the special moment when someone comes into
your world and you take pride in who you have
become. it is when you learn how to reciprocate
the exact feeling for them. it is when you form the
most cherished bond over conversations, which to
others may seem insignificant, but you know some
have the potential to change the last name.

she was always becoming something. most of the time, it was during the night when the world was asleep and her heart had time to talk with her mind about the things they cannot control. she was always becoming something. she pretended to be a doctor when she was a kid, running around saving everyone she could. she still does that now, but not as a profession. it is in her spare time where she puts back together pieces she keeps losing by trusting the wrong people. one day it will all make sense. one day the hurting will stop. one day the rain will wash her, instead of drowning who she is. she's always becoming something; a lion. a wolf. a unicorn. whatever it is, she's finding herself through the struggle and making beauty out of the quiet violence.

i come from the sea. my lungs are filled with ocean life and sand dollars. my hands hold waves that have not been born yet. my eyes are aquariums with the deepest parts of the oceans contained within them. my feet have a curious way about them, as they continue walking through the horizon and over mountains made of sand. my body tosses and turns, jonesing for another hit of light before i sink back into the wild blue. my lips kiss underneath the belly of every whitecap, tasting the salt i was made from. i have no idea what it would be like if i were anything else but the water surrounding me. the boats come and go. the birds fly over. the silence is never there long enough to know what i sound like. i am an outcast, but i am free.

the wax begins to drip onto you. in this moment, the flame reaches us both. we become the pleasure, pain, and adventure we have ached for since our eyes became fixated on what was beneath our skin. maybe we are disturbed or something entirely unique to this world. i would rather be authentically complex than live a life that isn't mine. i have never been into modern themes. some of me is old fashioned, though the parts you bring out are the carnivores i have had to tame from others in my past. i have no rules, but if you are to stay with me, you will have to learn how to listen to my movements before making your own. oddly made and uncovered after years of self-neglect, my actions are to please you every chance that finds us naked as water, or clothed as the strange humans we are.

she's a friend to everyone who tries their best to shine a light on those who need it. for wandering souls who find themselves in the gravity of her love, there is no such thing as being grounded to any one thing. just like the time flying around us, her strength is infinite. she takes a few moments each night to care for herself and make sure her energy is where it needs to be before resting her mind on tomorrow's chest. love doesn't always come at the right time, but i guarantee you, she will do her best at giving everything she has for whomever is willing to learn how the accumulation of heartache and heartbreak can only destroy you if you allow it. her presence doesn't come with a shadow. there is nothing she is running from. she imagined herself as someone who people could relate to in the time of struggle and victory. her mind rarely sleeps, though it feeds off of the negativity others try and place around her. she is a wanderlust who sips moon light underneath the grassy skies. an arrowhead made out of stars, she continues on with her life without worrying about judgment from those who will never understand her out of place laughter.

i honestly wonder if you know how beautiful you are and how you have made the oceans speak in waves. how you have made the sun lift the sky into morning. how you have given me the ability to believe someone like you actually sees me the way my mother saw me as a child. how when you let your hair down it deserves as a cue for the night to fall with it. i contemplate a thousand years worth of truths before approaching you. for me, if my body and soul are not aligned, i mercifully collapse upon the shadow's edge, where the living seek shelter from the dead. i wonder if you know how long it has taken me to put together my human parts to ask you one single question. i wonder if you have been standing there all this time with the crescent moon for a smile and thought about life like i do. with you, the wild lives on inside of every heart that never had a true chance to be heard, to be felt, to be loved.

one day, you will wake up and you will understand why things have happened this way. there was never anything wrong with you or how you loved or who you were. there was never anything wrong with the way you smiled at them or held them closer than midnight holds the stars. you will open your eyes one morning and realize they were not good enough for you. they were never supposed to stay in your life to the end. some humans briskly walk in and out like a summer's breeze in the middle of winter. one day you will move on from it all without ever looking back at what might have been and only live for the moments to come. they cannot have room in your heart which belongs to the chase. cowards love to stay there and feast on what is inside. i hope today is that day for you. i hope you come to terms with being more than what they offer. keep it open for an enormous love. a kind that will shift the universe for you to see yourself for the first time. it is where you belong. it is where life begins for the broken.

how you suffer is a reflection of who you are.
nothing ever takes the place of it. we just get
better at learning how to co-exist with it.
without its presence, we would not know
happiness. we would not value loss or
hardships. we would simply be inept at
breathing. suffering comes out of nowhere
like a storm surge with its hands together,
praying for destruction. once it leaves, you
are left with the remains. how you put it
back together directly depicts how you will
fair when the next one hits, because it will.
all of it is inevitable, which makes its teachings
worth more than thinking you can avoid it.
being prepared is beneficial, but acknowledging
there is a break in-between gives us our second
wind. the guidance of past failures exhumes the
truth of who we are. bones only tell a fragment
of the pain, when the ache is deeper than touch.

somewhere between the bones of tomorrow, i find myself sprawled out like a child, innocently searching for closure amongst the words unspoken and the ones that have been said. crawling out of the grave, i have been naked since the say i was born. my eyes still have dirt and earth inside them. my fingers massage the roots of flowers that have died, attempting to give them life and love. my back is curved with anxiety. my mind is glazed over with honey from bees trickling through rabbit holes i was mesmerized by. i pressed my mouth against the darkness and asked for forgiveness. to this day, i have not heard a murmur, but the silence is getting louder. maybe there is relief coming soon. my heart is sketched by fire, with flames breathing inside my lungs. somewhere between lies and truth, my knees stop shaking and can stand for the calling of something greater than where i am at currently. i cuss, howl, scream, and speak with fluidity as my jaw becomes unclenched. hinged on the idea of violence, i barely know the place where my head rests. once the skin crawls, i know i am getting closer to closure. we tend to forgive ourselves only when we have grown away from what and who we were before the tenderness could embrace the solitude we had been buried in. we are trying to find voices that do not belong to the bodies we inhabit, while deciphering the ones inside we habitually hear.

she has always been the little girl wearing all of the jewelry and sipping tea out of homemade cups. the imagination never leaves the princess who sees magic where others never look. maybe that's why she lives for the unexpected and walks where there are no roads. maybe that's why she gave up crying when her father never said goodbye. maybe that's why she still listens to sad songs to feel alive. when your pillow becomes your diary, your confessional, you learn how to survive differently. a picture is known to tell you things no one ever could, and that's why she no longer keeps them unless they are black and white. when the sky is peeled back, you will find her within the very fabric of what makes it a place of pureness and class. there are no secrets to be told by someone who dances around wearing only their soul. pay attention to the woman wearing it. she is never in the same place twice and makes damn sure her energy isn't being wasted. there is something to be said about how the earth moves below her. the reason why this is true, is because it has never touched her feet before.

you are all of my beautiful moments. you are all of
my mistakes and missed opportunities. you are the
lungs that have been drowned in water from those
who once said they would save me. you are the eyes
i have never had. you are the lining of truth in all
of the lies i ever told. you are the footprints on the
other side of the moon. you are the miracle and
disaster i thought would never know my touch.
you are a house with every door and window open,
allowing the wind to rush in to experience the
briefest of lifetimes to know what makes you feel
like the home it never had. you are the painted sky,
chipped and rustic, containing all of the universe's
secrets. in this life, love above anything else requires
sacrifice. always hold that in your heart with both
hands. it is more valuable than your sanity, because
there is a chance you can at least get that back.

first it will burn and you will think there isn't anything worth saving. then, one day, you will wake up and see how much it has changed you. a surrender of self occurs and you begin to finally see who you have always been through the eyes of those who have always seen you. a love is born from a death you never thought you could have survived. that is how warriors are created. that is where you take your first true step. that is where everything has a chance of killing you again, but you push through because it is what you need to do. do not get caught up in all of the bullshit people try and sell you on. it is only there for you to waste your time, and believe me, life is immensely better if you give more of it to the moments that matter and not base your happiness off of something being done out of guilt or spite. stay above your own mind and nurture it with self-servings of honesty. once you do, you will never be starved by another human offering you what they think will leave you satisfied.

i can be overly emotional or abundantly empty with everything i have in my life. it has been that way since i was a kid and didn't know how to write down all of my words. i expressed my unhappiness and confusion by crying out alone and drinking until my mind was swimming inside the bottle. i punched walls and burned things onto me. there was a time in my life when i used to harm myself. i never had anyone teach me how to handle who i was. my mother was always outside in the garage and my father was off working to make money to send home to us. i have notebooks that have never seen the light of day, because i am scared to go back and relive them. i look back at pictures of who i used to be and can see the emptiness in every one of them. it has taken me decades to get where i am today. i won't apologize for being over the top with how i feel. i see others who are content by walking with their heads down, looking for another exit. it takes me back to the boy who had a family, but always felt adopted to someone who never showed up. i can still remember the nights i had my cd player on and it would go through all five discs as i sat in bed, wondering if anyone else had to drown out the sounds around them or if they actually had the privilege of going to sleep without worrying about a door opening to scream at you because you were still up. my body is marked by moments that have made me appreciate the simple things life doesn't always offer to children who are different or unable to grasp what they did wrong to make everyone leave. those thoughts should never enter a child's mind, but nobody told me a goddamn thing about feeling alone at that age. my emotions are all over the writings and things i love. if it makes you uncomfortable, i am better now at people removing themselves entirely. after living and dying more times than most, i know the instructions have always been in people's actions. i am still all over the place with my thoughts and emotions, but it is centralized into a more conducive environment to thrive and not be left alone or behind this time.

we are the children of roses and the nectar of the gods. our bodies house an idea birthed by love and its meaning. there is no right way to express what you feel, but i fucking beg you, if you ever feel otherworldly about something, speak it out loud. too many of us go hungry for a conversation we have the power to start. you never know who will need it, but i promise you, someone out there right now is truly starving to hear you say something.

we are the love.

i could tell you all kinds of reasons as
to why i need you, but i know there isn't
one i could say that would keep you here
with me. i will forever look up and
admire your shine, wherever i am at.
if this is all we will ever become, may we
become the gods we were made to be.

i pointed up, then looked at her, and said, "home." there is no other explanation for the light beaming out of her cracks. she used to tell me how jealous she was of mine, but that was before life got in the way of us and handed her obstacles she was willing to bleed for. she is my armor, my shield, my ever sharpened sword. she is a battle i will fight alongside, if it means there is a chance of going to die for her.

i just wanted to get to know you, but silence is
still all that is familiar about you to me. i need
my peace and you need your life. sometimes,
goodbye isn't even needed. all we can do is
turn our heads again, and walk away.
after that, may the sunsets bring us back.

i will never ask for now.
i just want it to be you
when the angel of death
comes looking for where
my love goes. we will
fight it together, until the
devil himself surrenders his
thrown for the broken he
has condemned to his flames.

i miss a lot of things these days. far too many to name off, but there is one in particular that nestles itself inside of my mind and keeps me up with every star. the freckle on your left side, right above your hip. to think i have touched magic before will always keep me up, wishing for more to find me again, someday.

i used to be a lot of things others never understood.
it wasn't until i heard your name that i knew who i
was. it wasn't until you touched me that i felt
human. it wasn't until you held me that i knew
what my heart was meant for.

proving everything means nothing if you are not doing it for yourself. i wanted to be the best student, but i let alcohol stop me. i wanted to be the best athlete, but i let alcohol stop me. i wanted to be the best Marine, but i let alcohol stop me. i want to be the best writer, and nothing is going to stop me. life begins to make sense again once you become your own vice, your own voice, your own truth.

i may not need you as i did before, but i still think of
you as if you are the one i want to build a life with.
i fell in love five times yesterday. each time, i closed
my eyes. it was then i saw and felt you looking at
me. love is the place where soul strengthens a
single connection between two humans who
swear they have lived a life before this one.
it is where hearts and bones complete a
stranger who was never one to begin with.

i am not looking for you to replace the emotions
and love i have lost. i am simply after a moment
with you, which turns out to be the last thing my
memory consists of. i know we have dreams to
dream, but as long as your eyes close with mine,
my heart can be easily found next to yours.
it can be unquestionably conquered by
the spirit living within yours.

be brave for me and i will be brave for you.
love is nothing more than being able to be
around someone who wants to know the
parts no one else has been able to get
to see, understand, and adore.

i wish i meant as much to you as you do to me.
i thought you wanted to live for me, but in the
end, it is who you choose to die with that sets
us free. i am just a bird now, with wings
waiting on a permanent breeze.

there you are, whispering to stormy winds
and carrying mighty seas. be still, sweet
angel. tomorrow tells us to be patient for
what today is teaching us. we are only half
of who we are when the day awakes us.
we are only full when darkness swallows
its shadow to bring us light.

we are all broken during some point in
our lives. my cracks have names and faces
i do not care to give power to anymore,
but i must recognize they have made me
who i am. be water, be oceans, be courage,
be godly, be wild, be adventurous, be whatever
you need to become in order to visualize you
are not like the rest. your power comes from
being able to love despite your fault lines.
step, move, and breathe easy, child. you are
safe in the arms of your own for now.

there were places on the map we never got to,
but love found us before we were ready. it is still
here, still breathing, still able to linger longer than
a star can burn. a life means nothing if you are not
prepared to spend it fighting for every fucking
thing you cannot live without. so here i am
without you, but maintaining my purpose of
fire and fight to get back to you and the moon
within you. my shine is only for your eyes.

i am in love with someone i cannot even be with.
if there is such a thing as death, it is knowing you
will never know their love to be anything more than
an idea, a feeling, a casket slowly closing on your
body, suffocating whatever was left from a life spent
dying to be closer to them. it is right before fresh
earth is spread on top of you, do you feel alive
for a brief second to know love lives on outside
of the body you once thought never knew
what its name actually was. lights flicker
and you are home once again.

i will keep talking to the moon about you until
her light becomes something we both can share.
until she is living with us for all of the time we
have left together. our life's story will be a million
little more secrets she keeps for souls dressed as
humans playing their part in a play where tragedy
is magic and death is the only act that's read.

teach me, and reach for me when you feel weary.
live for me and i will write for you until words
become a touch only you can feel. i have missed
you since the first time you kissed me. i have loved
you since the second right before your eyes found
mine. there is no me in this world without you.
i am here, because your breath still sits on the
moon, giving life to her light.

sunsets make everything worth it. they give
me closure to an ending i was unprepared
for. they give me a love i was born without.
they give me purpose for a color living
within me that had been neglected
my entire life. they tell me it is okay
to slow down and enjoy the last few
moments of a love not always
destined to survive. red has never
meant more to me than when
it shines on you.

once before, when i was a boy, the moon told me to never lose hope in the ones i love. once before, when i was a teenager, the moon told me to start loving myself more, because humans can kill you with their lies if you allow them. once before, when i was fighting for my life, the moon came down and told me to trust in the light that had once washed over the skies and now dances freely in your eyes. i have listened to the moon my entire life and not once has she left without saying goodnight. not once has she ever left without telling me she would be back. she told me about that night when i was a boy, and now i am talking to her about you. we do not always trust things we cannot see or feel, but i never believed in much until i met you. all it took was me understanding how trust is what our minds and hearts fight over, when in the end, it is our soul that needs it the most.

when someone strong has everything taken away
from them, it takes an even stronger human to
bring them back. they do not need half of what
they once had. all they need is for the person
to laugh a little and smile. the effort is always
noticed, because of how difficult it is trying to
give them a feeling they have never had before.
it is not easy, and at times, it is an all out war
with yourself. but you do it because they matter.
humans who have been through the fire know
each other well. you can always tell by the way
they hold onto things a little tighter than most.
especially when it comes to love. you must
find something out of the thousands of things
pulling you under to hold onto in order to get
back on your feet. people think life is out to
get them, but in reality, we are after everything
we cannot have. there is a time and place for
all of us. at the end of the day, the best thing
you can do, is go after anything that moves
you to be a better human.

true healing takes time. there is no right or
wrong way to get there. sometimes it is a dark
room without windows and starving yourself
from what you need. other times it is waking
up with the sun and gutting it up, regardless
of the pain. it is a tough and muddy road.
there will be times you'll think your feet
cannot move another step, but you will
get through it, because you are made up
of gold and galaxies, much more complete
than how you currently feel. do not collapse
into your own sorrow. learn to grow from it
and become a reason why someone else tries
their hardest to overcome the ache you finally
beat into submission by persevering when
you   could have folded up with your doubts.
we keep living, because we must. if you are
persistently trying to sabotage your mindfulness
with negativity draped over you, blocking out
anything resembling progress and change,
your existence will only create more longing
for needless suffering. be a friend to your
heart and soul. as lonely as you feel, things
are exponentially compounded when the
human forgets self-love and turns on itself.

i simply want someone to hold onto during the night. it gets increasingly lonely spending time with your own thoughts that remind you how abandoned you actually are once the moon forgets your name. i get tired of begging and pleading for someone to love me. i get more hopeless as the days go by and no one is there for me when my soul returns back to my body empty handed once again. maybe i am trying too hard for my own good. love is nothing more than suffocating the darkness inside of you. i want you too much for you to not want me at all, and that is a painful lesson to keep learning after all of these years. we will never receive what and who we need, until we believe we are enough to satisfy our own company and the demons we keep.

being broken led me to light again.
it showed me how the shore is
only safety if you do not choose
to chase the waves. even then,
you are risking your life for
a lighthouse who neglected to
shine for you after being lost
at sea for half your life, thinking
your limbs could hold up and
carry you back to a fresh start.

maybe it wasn't what she said that scared you the most, but the way she said it. there is gravity in her soul that pulls you in when you had been looking for a place to call home. she's not quiet about anything she does. it isn't meant to be in an obnoxious way. being around such a force will leave you looking inside of yourself to see what you have left. she is not concerned about the feelings you have for the way she conducts her life, because it took her years to become confident enough to live again. certain people know who they are and what they can offer. she is at a point in her journey where being happy is no longer a fairy-tale. women like her are born from the grave where people desperately tried to bury them. silencing someone for the sake of winning an argument can be a death blow to many, but here she is, surviving it all. be cautious with those who hold back their voice. for they will ultimately hold back their love for you and cause you to walk this earth with your heart showcased as a reminder that even silence can have a name and place to live and breathe.

your heart and head on my chest. it is the only way
i know how to breathe without losing what is left of
me. i hold you and i have all the love i have ever lost.
you came back to me once before. i can only hope
you find your way back to a man who is still
trying to find himself. a man who is
still lost to a sunrise made up of your
lightning smile and golden bones.

you are love and all its glory and madness.
i am speechless when it comes to enunciating
my pain now. it has since exited my life and
followed my demons along with it. you are
the sweetest breath and most beautiful
structure my hands have ever had the
pleasure of touching. what an emerging
sensation you are. what a shimmering
turn of fate you have become.

this year has taught me who i am and who i am not. it taught me how to have forgiveness for who i was and who others showed themselves to be. lessons can be people and certain ones will never fit into your life, no matter how much it pains you to remove them. change is the only constant thing in our lives, and without it, we would never evolve into the version we need for ourselves. hearts break, but we have the power to love regardless of the state they are in. pain is inevitable and hope only visits those worthy enough to admit it. life isn't out to get you. it is there to remind you what you still need to accomplish. this year, you will meet people you never dreamed could enter your life. trust yourself more. there is no reason to make a list if you never mark anything off. allow your intuition to guide you, but never paralyze you. being tired is a lousy excuse and a lazy mindset for not wanting to do something that has the potential to change your life. welcome the uncomfortable situations. they make it easier for you to do the impossible. breathe in a few more times. i mean really fucking breathe for once. loosen your lungs and let it all go. laugh louder. worry only if it matters. location isn't forever. adventure out of your safe space and get a few more bruises from the wildest forms of exploring. may your setbacks become your motivation to believe in all things extraordinary. my wish for you all is that you set as many goals as you can, even if you do not reach them all. i wish for your heart to remain full on whatever and whomever you love. i wish for your hands to never be empty. i wish for your pockets to be always full of all kinds of things besides money. i wish for your happiness to not be predicated on someone else. i wish for your lowest moment isn't upon the floor. if it is, just know it is where miracles can occur. i only hope if you find yourself there, it is rolling around with someone you love and cannot live without, acting like the kids you are. may this year be the year you have been waiting on your entire life. may today be the day that changes everything and allows you the opportunity to seek out and find the steps you never could take before.

i am doing my best moving on and burying all of
the little moments we had. baby steps never felt
more like crawling than it does now. but i am
going to keep digging my fucking fingers into
this earth, making my mark and leaving bruises
where you left them on me. i am not worried
about healing and getting over you. i have done
it all before, before you. i can only wish you the
best and hope whatever pain you caused me,
finds you during quiet moments where you feel
as if you are over me. you brought the devil out in
me again. this time though, hell is walking with me.
i know what dying feels like, and this is not that.
i am just stepping into the man i need to be in
order to get over someone who used to hold me
and tell me it would be okay. i finally believe in my
own words today. today, i feel content in shooting
out the sun and staying up with the moon.

though i am incomplete, i am still whole. when i was growing up and finding my way through this life, i tried replacing what i had lost by collecting pieces of those who said they loved me. it turns out, you need someone who actually means it or else you become shadows and dust of an abandoned youth. there is no blame to give other than to myself for the way life has transpired up until the point of meeting you. i was the victim of my own murder. i was the boy who cried with wolves and got lost in his addictions. i was the man who fucked up anything that felt like love. there wasn't a part of me worth the skin it was covering. useless, nameless, and forgotten was a mindset i fought years to embrace. today, i find you with my hands walking miles all over your body. today, i wake up wrapped up in a dream with long black hair who finds protection in me. today, i am whole. if someone were to ever ask me what love is and what it means to me, i would look at them with my entire heart showing through my eyes, and tell them, "it is when my body searches for warmth and she is who it finds."

i took some time this evening to press my ear to the
sky and listen to the universe. chaos calms me and
i know it is one of the reasons why i am still alive.
hearing how the slightest vibration can bend the
universe above me, it is then i see how powerful
appreciation actually can be. i love everything for
the most part and some things more than i should.
i have always been that way and it has put me in
precarious situations, but i would not change them.
my ear is still pressed firmly against the light above
me, trying to feel its pulse, as it beats for more love.
grow for the cosmos and it will feed you and give
you everything you need. it is plentiful for those
who are in touch with the soul of what surrounds
them. visualize yourself at a point in your life where
you are no longer making excuses for what you did.
where there is no one else to blame for being
unreasonable and disgusted at what you see inside.
begin at the spot where it hurts the most and follow
the pain until you are covered in a self-discovered
truth where we control all of what comes and goes
in our lives. all of the misery, love, heartache,
suffering, rejection, and acceptance, is ascertained by
welcoming who we are and knowing who we are not.

people will judge you relentlessly because you do
not conform to the way they perceive life to be.
you might as well keep to your side of crazy.
give them something to tell their friends about
and make this life worth a damn for yourself.
it doesn't get any easier if you make friends or
you don't. you never know which face they will
show the next day when they need something
from you or you are in need of them. look out
for yourself and do things that make you dance
when everyone else is afraid to walk because of
the unknown. there is not a single reason to let
others impact how you live your life. let them be
the fools who are jealous of the light you brought
to the table and now walking away with. whatever
happens, please do not give them satisfaction of
thinking they are better off without you. humans
can be lame creatures and oftentimes, fall back
onto their egos to see who will catch them.
be wanderlistic amongst the ordinary. happiness
lies within the fingertips of those who touch magic
others swear to be make-believe.

when i think about it, the saddest day of my life will be the day my voice leaves me and i will not be able to tell you, "i love you." hopefully i have thrown enough of who i am into the universe before i go and it finds you wherever you are. maybe then you will see how i could never leave you. i want you to go through life happy and not necessarily forgetting about me, but remembering what we had when you have those days where you think unbearable is what you must live with. the memory of me should never hold you back from achieving the life you want, sweet love. dance, laugh, and drink your wine. fall for everything your heart jumps at. be the woman who scaled mountains to pick flowers at the top. be the woman who gave her time freely to anything and anyone who looked like an adventure. be the woman who could make the dullest of things memorable by simply showing up. when i think about the greatest day of my life, it was when our eyes caught each other and relived the love we had before that moment. before you, i often wondered if someone was out there who could make sense of me. now i know without any hesitation she will continue changing the world, one twirl of her hair at a time.

the worst kind of heartache there is, is the kind you never think you will come back from. if you are reading this and feel this way or have felt this way, you will understand there is a possibility of it happening again. time does not heal earthquakes and we are undeniably changed forever. it is how we love the next that brings us back to life for the better. we cannot feel sorry for ourselves when there is more to do in life than expecting everything working out like you imagined it would. we are artists at heart and need every experience to craft our gifts. take whatever you feel, gently hold it, and seek out the next dare you have been hiding from. the cure will be found in the things your mind has stopped you from believing in. destiny happens when you open yourself up to the pain and embrace the mess of it all. only then will you be able to know who you are.

i do not want to wake up one day and feel as if i have never lived. regret is the kind of death you hear about, and until it happens to you, you really have no fucking idea how to reverse it. you spend hours contemplating what if, which spirals into days then multiplies into months and divides your years into stages that ultimately lead you nowhere. i do not want to wake up and not have the strength to change my mind, when i know getting out of bed earlier will lead me to more ideas and experiences. i do not want to wake up and not have the chance to get in my vehicle and drive where wild meets crazy with open arms. i do not want to die before i get to you with this feeling i have now for adventure. i do not want to breathe in stories from someone else, when i had the opportunity to do the same thing. we place value on things, without money, we could never afford. but there are always free memories we pass on, because we say we are busy or we will get to them later. there is no later. there is now, and i hope you make it out of your comfort zone to know how it feels not to miss something. how it feels to be entirely present instead of absent from your own dreams. i hope you have your eyes open long enough to feel the piercing impact love can have on you once you give yourself a chance to roam as far as your wings can take you. saying no to what ignites your soul, only leaves you crawling around, looking for more excuses. life is about overcoming your fear of failing. i hope you go mad for it all.

there isn't much left of who i was before meeting you. we change only if it suits them for the most part these days, which is sad, because stubbornness gets in the way of an extraordinary amount of priceless moments we end up sacrificing for no reason. you will lie to yourself and say how much you are better off being you, being this version, when you have no idea how it feels to be anyone other than somebody who ends up being alone. there are no easy paths to take when trying to figure this thing out. we were made to change and adapt to our given situations based on what is going on around us. maybe one day you will give someone more than what you are accustomed to giving. maybe one day you can feel what it is like being vulnerable and satisfied by allowing yourself the small pleasures of life. i hope you can open yourself up to the possibility long enough to catch the light others are willing to show you. it is okay to be scared. it is okay to show feelings. it is okay to give up the safety of your own hiding spot to step into someone else's. the monsters will not find you. the voices will go silent. you do not have to keep all of that to yourself. it is okay to let it all fall at your side and move forward with your heart in your hands. is there a chance of getting hurt and your stitches opening up, yes, but i do not want to arrive at my final resting place unscathed. i want there to be stories, laughter, pain, and a steady dose of boldness written all over me. with you, my soul swells with anticipation. i know i have made it when i look at you. i know there is risk in each and every breath taken, and yet, i still find safety in the chaos we create.

you are all consuming cosmos.
you see me by caring for me
and giving my soul a voice.
my mind is alive and remains
lit with feverish flames for you.
before my words tell your story,
your breath gives my breath
reason to exist. without you
here with me, my flesh would
walk away from me, using
my backbone as a cane to
make sense of whatever pain
was here before your showed
me what grace and adoration
can look like in human form.

i don't know what others think success is or means
these days. most of the time i feel like a failure for
everything i have done to sabotage my own life.
other times, i cannot believe i am still alive and
able to do what i love to do. that is success to me.
waking up and knowing you get to do what you love.
knowing no one else can or ever will replicate your
abilities and dreams. it is more than a singular realm
of transparency. it is to awake an enlightening
pursuit of excellence. i know my life is not where
i want it to be right now. maybe yours is not either.
but that should not discourage us from trying to
better ourselves. this year has taught me many things.
most importantly, it has given me time to reflect on
what i need and do not need in my life. it has given
me a new found fight to maintain my balance of art
and love. a place where both live and breathe in the
same meaning.

i always see your heart in the clouds.
people ask me why i look up as often
as i do at something they never see for
themselves. i do not say a word. if i
should ever speak about it, i would
disturb the only loving thought and
idea i have the entire day. my peace
means more to me now that you are
gone, but still ever so close to the
human lining of what keeps my
bones from falling out
of my flesh.

maybe you can see the scars where life tried to tear you apart. maybe you can feel where it took out your heart and replaced it with a universal sized hole. maybe you can feel the earthquake shaking what remains of your bones. maybe you can see the eyes that remember every face and color that has crossed their path. maybe you can see the dreams through each crack in the skull where you have fallen down a flight of stars too many times, hoping there would be something there to catch your wandering mind. maybe you can feel the hands that have lost touch of reality and left to hang at your side to never glide over a body that burned for your love. losing it all made you gain an appetite that desires new places to visit and humans to interact with. the ones we met along the way prior to this phase of life had a weird way of showing they cared. they looked only to see what was wrong and not what was going right. i have failed honestly, lovingly, and for most of the time, alone. i was only good at getting the minimum life had to offer. though there were those rare occasions when i even surprised myself at the amount of achievements i had earned. none of them really made me happy. i am humble to a fault and almost a detriment to myself, but i do not see why i need to be congratulated for doing the right thing or doing what i love. it is like when you go to work and you truly care about things you are doing, you will never have to work a day in your life. that has been true for a lot of moments throughout this journey of mine. more specifically, towards the one i adore. love should not be work. love should just be. i understand you will have days where it doesn't feel that way. but if it is what you want, then it shouldn't be the only thing keeping you up at night when they are away from you. for a second, minute, or fucking hours at a time, allow the feeling to remind you why you are putting your heart into the dreams you live.

i think about you, because i want to know what it is like spending the day with you and walking with you. i think about looking into your eyes and seeing something more than a reflection of loss. i think about you, because it feels like it is supposed to be this way. i think about holding your hand and feeling what you feel and what your soul has felt ever since it entered your body and gave you life. i want to learn it and where it came from so i can pinpoint the exact moment your love entered the atmosphere and gave mine reason to find my body. i think about laying next to you and feeling your energy and presence next to me. i think about you, because in all honesty, i have not thought about anyone like this in over eight years. i think about you, because it makes me feel human again.

when you say you have all of the issues and i do not, i think you forget how long it has taken me to get to this point in my life. i am still fucked up. i still have flashbacks. i still hear voices. i still see shit that is not even there. my sanity is not everyone else's. i adore you for who you are and what you have been through. with all of that being said, i imagine i am at least ten years too late getting to you. i hope you were able to drift to safe place and find peace last night, sweet moon. you are the most fucking beautiful, thoughtful, and thought provoking wanderlust i have ever walked with. i swear on the stars i have held you before. it is the only way i can make sense of this familiarity. my own happiness has taken a backseat to a lot of my friendships over the years. i am self-sacrificing, and in return, i get my heart fucking smashed in on all four sides. i am bruised with lies and whatever else wishes to take its shot at me. i am an over-emotional, obsessively protective, understanding, caring, and hyper-vigilant about the things i have and need. my heart and soul do not know any other way to coexist as one. this is how i will love you if you allow me to live within your universe. this is how i will miss out on death itself, by caring for your youthfulness in abundance.

i am going to close my eyes now. i hope you fall into a dream that catches you with its soul. may those dreams cover your bones in the most unforgettable colors. i hope you find a breath that keeps you smiling to be alive under a sky of a million moons staring back into your eyes. i hope you are able to lay down in a field of stardust and feel how you were put together so lovingly.

life is made to be loved. if you ever find yourself doubting it, may you feel the universe's heartbeat within you. may you never falter or stumble on your way up. you are a dove amongst ravens. you are picasso's favorite color. please remember your worth when others around you are feeling worthless. you are not one of them. catch the breeze and fly on, sweet child.

"doing your best to get through it."

i remember you telling me that when i would ask you how your day was going. it still rings true for me to this day. with every possible action we make and take on in life, it heals me. i admire your wisdom and perspective, not just with my own shit, but with life in general. we all must hurt before we heal and even after that, it is going to fucking hurt, because those people who ended up in our lives, create a cornerstone that will never be touched by anyone else, regardless of how amazing they are. the Facebook memories are super tough to see. i saw some wild ones the other day which had me crying and breaking down, but i also saw how far i had come since those days. i thank you for sharing things like you do with me. i know you hate it when i say "thank you," but it is all i know how to say sometimes. i can only hope it is a reminder to you of how amazing you are, not only as a woman, but a mother to your children. they are better because of you and the love you've kept alive.

running away with you will be my greatest adventure.
we will slip through the night, like waves escaping
the light. on we go, on we love. we are the lines the
stars will trace. we are the humans that every
other soul will remember when there is nothing
left of this place except gravestones and
dead flowers. we are love's greatest epiphany.

when i was a kid, i always had this feeling of wanting to do more and helping someone who everyone seemed to dismiss. i knew then, probably by age six, the world was going to be cruel and unforgiving to a large majority of humanity. i never understood pain the way others did. how they relentlessly went after those who were deemed weaker or unworthy, day after day, without feeling any sense of remorse for being worthless themselves. the pain i knew and became familiar with growing up, taught me how to never indulge in such brutality against a soul. i have over the course of my life been guilty a few times of thinking i was better than someone else. thinking i deserved more and could do more with what others had. when i was eight, i began feeling that i would never make it to see my 30th birthday. i do not know if that is a common conception for kids who knew nothing about the life ahead of them. all throughout my years of being here, i fell victim to my own thoughts and almost sabotaged my journey by drinking and taking drugs to combat my demons and depression. looking back, i should have died a thousand times over, but hopefully i have saved what life i had in time to make amends for what i did to myself and those i hurt in the past. growing up being an empath, i struggled daily to survive. the feelings of others were embedded into my own and it nearly cost me everything. i self-imploded a million times, but i never passed off my pain and anger to anyone , nor did i blame them. not even my parents felt it when they split up. i took it all out on myself. all of the screaming, yelling, and dysfunction, i created a world within it. being me now, i still have days where i find it damn near impossible to believe i am still alive. the empathy has given me perspective now, and what i have done with it, i am very proud of. you do not need to know someone to understand their pain. you do not need to belittle someone because the are not like you. i am ashamed and angered by those who do. i can only hope you figure it out before you are withering away in what you perceive to be a good life.

i hope you never surrender your passion for exploring all facets of who you are and what you need from life. i hope you continue exercising your right to travel and speak about things you love and crave from those whom you let into our heart. i hope the road you find yourself on is full of enchanted detours and views no one else can give you. i hope you can be enough for yourself when everyone else is loitering beside an idea or dream they cannot seem to chase. i hope you take advantage of every obstacle you will face, because there will be those who force you to walk back any part of progress for the simple fact of being content with what they already possess. i hope you find your eyes meandering along the horizon where all of life is created, to finally understand you belong here and you in fact do matter to this unforgiving blue cue ball of magic. maintain your beliefs, and if you find anything, i hope you meet a few humans who bring out the impossible in you.

when someone you want to be with cannot embrace
the love you offer, you need to reconsider what you are
looking for when it comes to love. you need to know not
everyone will be able to hold what you are caring to give.
it doesn't define what you are worth. sometimes, we need
to be alone to value ourselves more. sometimes, we
need our lungs to grow into the body they are
housed in before attempting to use somebody else's
for resuscitation. being rejected for what you want to
hand out freely, only means you will be someone
others look to when their life supply
is low. comprehend the difference between acceptance
of self and acceptance of remedial opportunity being
thrown out in a last ditch effort for someone to save
whatever is left of their heart. some humans are born
with it inside of their chest. others go through life
being born with it in their hands. hold onto it for as
long as you can and remember how empty it feels once
it is gone. do not lose yourself in order to find someone
who only cares about the collection amassing on the
shelves they have made out of the lonely. being kind
means the vulnerability side of life is the most important
thing to you. if you go seeking for another who feels this
way, your heart will be protected as if it is the grandest
of treasures ever discovered by a single entity seeking
commitment. there are those out there who love to
simply love someone else and those who love to lose
themselves altogether, no matter the cost. each one
demands a certain price in the end. i hope you save
enough for yourself if something should ever happen.

i was designed by sin to never forget where i came from.
my curse is only that to those whom wish to see me as
one of their own, before seeing me as an individual.
my only mistake has been believing i was never good
enough for the happiness i was deprived of as a kid.
when you are twelve years old and having to console
your mother breaking down in the garage over lost love,
you feel it is only right to tell her you still love her and
everything is going to be okay. even if the tears do not
stop. the pain still trembles through your bones. the
anxiousness is born and given a proper name.
you think you are doing what a real man would do.
life teaches you lessons on how to provide the necessary
for those who are incapable of healing on their own. life
also teaches you to be judicious with your energy and time,
because not everyone deserves the two things we barely have
left over for ourselves after dying before our lips declare love
for someone worthy of what we always give to others. some
people are raised by misguidance and others stay lost forever.
i have made countless excuses in the past for who i was, but
as i got older, i realized some humans are just made to be a
type of darkness to defend the true light in others. we are
protectors for those who cannot see their own. we feel the
universe differently than most, but it doesn't mean we are
foreign to the neglect we oftentimes feel when we are young,
and even more so when we age with the earth. some things
cannot be forgotten, which is why we tend to go back to the
start in order to find a new truth about who we really are.
i am only here to discover new ways to love, live, and learn.
anything else is a reward i will pass down to those who are
still looking for where they belong.

your love has always been a fucking dream of mine.
it has always been a universe full of magical whispers
and gentle moans. it will always be the most peaceful
thing i awake to. i am here. i get to be here. i am not
leaving from this spot until you take what you need
and i can return the favor. i am going to need to
show you how it feels to have your eyes roll back
inside of your fucking skull, staring at another
dimension you wish to live in. you may grip the
sheets if you must, but they will not save you
from moving with me and the currents we make.

i was always looking for the next escape. some drug or drink that could save me. somebody or something to hold me. i was a lost boy, hell bent on killing whatever was in me that made me such a chaotic human. i found a place where i can rest without worrying about those i cannot help. i found a place where it welcomes me with love and acceptance, regardless of how my day went. it keeps me happy and guilt free from the bystanders lurking through fences someone tried to use to separate child from parent. to separate thought from dream.

maybe there is enough of me to give to someone else. at times, it is such a chore loving myself, but i know there is a love out there for me. there must be a way to get to you before our opportunity runs its course without giving you what you deserve. love is nothing more than an absence of you now.

you never realize the amount of time you are
unhappy, when you have been pretending for so
long that you were to simply pass the day. one day,
you will look into the mirror and see yourself eighty
and alone, perhaps. i sincerely hope you make the
best out of this life before it makes you callous and
scorned with hate you will birth and carry around
like the unborn child you are.

the tv is on, but muted. i would much rather hear
these keys typing than listen to the world and what
they are trying to sell me. my peace comes from the
chaos i create when i am alone and able to see
myself as the man i always knew i could be
once i finally heard forgiveness in my silence.

this place will try and break the softness you keep.
protect it, and it will keep you from becoming like
those who were unsure of who to become when the
darkness devoured their light.

may you find what you are looking for while
reading these words. just know it is okay to
be unwell and crazed with wild. it is okay to
be pissed off and upset about something not
going your way. it is okay to cry and want to
be alone. it is okay to be everything these
humans do not understand. you are here
now and one day you won't be. you must
take full advantage of this certainty. it is
okay not to be okay, but do not allow it to
ruin and run your life. use it and create the
art this earth needs. your voice and dreams are
valuable. if not to anyone else, they are to me.

learn to appreciate the moment before it turns into
another memory you end up replaying in your mind,
hoping the ending changes. there is no other death
quite like regret. it is something that will keep
your soul in chains long after your body
has left this godforsaken place of horrors.

i am always fascinated by those who choose to eat
alone in restaurants. they remind me to be happy
and help me learn more about who i am. they are
content with being that way and i am content
dining alone. i enjoy watching other people be
themselves. you can learn a lot just by paying
attention to where their eyes and hands
go after they are done eating.

may your next breath be the one that knocks out
any doubt residing in your heart. may it be the
awakening it needs to rest and find strength to
beat again and again. may it be every living
moment you are alive to make. glory rides
on like new love being evinced.

i feel like i am losing you. i feel like i am lost without
you. it feels like you are gone. i feel like you do not
need me anymore. i feel like you have already left.
i feel like you now. confused and alone has
never felt like home to me. though tonight,
my body has only enough room to hold
onto what you made me.

all we need is for someone to never forget why we
chose them. all we need is love, love, sweet love.
maybe it comes in the form of a human. maybe it
comes in the shape of a new day. tomorrow waits
for only you to grow out of who you are today.
i hope your shedding continues.

there is not enough air i could hold in my lungs to
give you what you need. there are only shards of soul
left. i am learning how to pick each one out so i can
understand the life it had and its meaning for
breaking as it did. my soul is sol. i have dreams
of burning with a love like that. i have feelings of
freeing the wild entity within me. i have a snuggled
promise to remain beside her, and only her. sweet
convictions kiss my bones. it is only then i feel my
own strength for life. it is only then i feel my own
remorse for the death i am responsible for.

to love you is to know how close one can actually get
to the moon without stepping foot onto her precious
soil. you are the piece of earth i will always cling to
when the ground beneath me begins to give way.
you are the flower i will look at and imagine
being a million drops of rain to water its roots.
to love you, is to know there is still a reason
for being this way when it comes to caring
for something greater than myself.

there is a subtle ease about her that calms my soul
long enough to realize i have never known love and
love has never known me, until now. there is a storm
brewing outside. you can smell the lightning about to
kiss earth. i can taste the sex on your skin. i was
born a wild beast, and i will love you as i am.

be with love and nothing will break you. be with who
you are and no one can replace it. be with the moon
and stay wildly in love with it all. looking out of my
window, i have alien-like eyes. this world is quite
confusing to someone not from here. oftentimes,
i am finding more reasons why i love my solitude
and why i am more productive on my own. i can
hear better. i am thinking without feeling anyone
else. my introvertive and empathetic abilities
thrive off of it. all of me is mine.

being here keeps me honest, which makes my writing authentic. i believe in everything that pours out of me, but it is more relatable once i have removed reality from my world. it is the reason you should write. it is the only fucking reason. anything else and you are cheating yourself a story that is
not yours to tell.

some day i may die alone, but i will have known the
greatest love story ever told. it will be buried or
burned with me. i shall keep it inside of my soul
for it to be planted in the galaxy we choose to
call home when you come back to me.
homesickness is anywhere without you.

we are all strangers to the wild we keep
we are all lovers to the chaos we make.
we are all lost to a calling. we are all
in love with someone who cannot
love us back. life is only boring if
you continually choose to ignore the
beauty and ache set out before you.

if i am not moving, it feels like i am allowing my demons to catch me. i am not running towards anything if i am being honest. i just need space from everything at times. i just need to know i am safe without needing anyone else. i am a concoction of nerves, bones, and fear. on my good days, i am humanly able to forget what it feels like to feel anything at all.

i live with anxiety, ptsd, and depression.
they are   diseases and can be treated.
those who know this pain, this terrible
cell of flames, may believe they are incurable.
there is always a foot in/foot out approach.
a flight/fight sort of perception. our job is to
find the balance to withstand the rigors of hell
it all puts us through. it is something i am not
scared to admit or talk about openly. i can
find resolve without needing more than what
they are giving me. there is a way out that
doesn't involve numbing it. there is a way that
doesn't involve ending a life that is still mighty
and ready to begin again. i found it. i am
sending good light and love to you so you can
see it, too.

i do not plan my life. i go where the energy directs me. my life may not be suitable for others, but i fucking love going where answers are left for you to find. you must initiate all of the magic. that is the trick. that is the rabbit we chase.

my mind is an endless labyrinth filled with growing stories that have not drank the universe or had a taste of sweet mercy before. they sit idle with anticipation to develop into something that will be able to sustain the integrity of hope.

and when dawn breaks, i hope it doesn't break you.
i hope it stays a while so it can get to know the dusk
of who you are. there is potential for a miracle
as long as you understand sacrifice goes both
ways if you are after the same things as the
one you are with. balance keeps the mind
and heart from falling away from center.
it all starts with who you allow to help you
with your own fears of doing the same thing.

sing your words to the masses. sing as loudly as you can. suffocate the hate raging war around you. your truth should mean more than pretending to be another lyric to someone else's favorite song.

it is eight thirty-three in the evening. a few more humans are pulling into the hotel. there are a few scattered humans across the eating establishments. the night is approaching with her stars, and i am anxiously awaiting her to lift up her skirt to show me love. i am awaiting the greatest display of life on earth.

i close my eyes that have seen too much to be this
fucking young. they are jaded, but i am too whole
to give in and sleep. there are copious amounts of
light to be touched. to be felt by these hands which
remain steady gliding down your back, shoulders,
and the front of your body to firmly hold
your breasts. they remember how you once
moved for me. i can only remember and
smile in anticipation for the next time
it hears my commands again.

i sit here not knowing anything more than the color
of the sky will forever change as the day ends. maybe
that is all i need to know. maybe that is all there is.
if true, it is a goddamn fire show and i have the
best seat in the entire state. there is no other kind
of love, if not love as kind as enlightenment.

as the night welcomes in its travelers, i embrace all that was today. i kiss it on the forehead, and thank it by seeing the third eye of who today was. may it bring me a tomorrow i can love just as much.

we fall victim to our own expectations more times
than not. balance is the only thing keeping my legs
from giving up. it is the only separation my heart
and mind can comprehend.

the only people i want to be around are those who have bled for their dreams. those who continue to stay weird. those who remain broken or who have had second thoughts about the journey we find ourselves on. they make me think, love, and accept this reality for whatever we damn well choose it to be. i crave soul in all things. i crave not meaning, but a defined calling to this madness.

there is wild withering away inside of you. take time
to care for it. it will lead you to the edge of earth
where all things are free to drink the stars.
it will guide you to a face as familiar as
the one holding yours with their love.

there are only so many days and minutes in a year to express my soul to you. in time, i shall tear down the skies for you and bring you the rain, thunder, fire, and angels. by the time i am done, our world will be entirely made for you and i. there is nothing worth fighting for, if not for complete brilliance.

i woke up at six fifteen this morning, craving the
sunrise. it did not disappoint. each color, vibration,
and particle of energy was consumed properly. i am
a walking human, full off of morning delight.
there you will find the immaculate fullness of life.

you showed me how to love my pieces as much as the entirety of who i was. some treasures in life can only be found after they become broken and forgotten about. those are the ones you should continue loving. even if they are lost for years, you will never mistake their value or misjudge their price.

for the first time since i have been here, i am alone on this side of the hotel. freedom is not where you find yourself without others. it is where you find yourself surrounded by the company you love; humans, places, feelings, moments, zero expectations.

my mission in life is to help those i can, while i can.
if i am not able to do so, the pain grows on giving
trees i have placed. each leaf that falls, is a reminder
i did not give it enough water or sources of energy to
sustain its maturity. i must remind myself that i, too,
need the same nutrients to be me; to remain alive.

being in love means allowing the one you are with to continue transforming into who they were going to be before you. what their life was going to look like. what their eyes were going to say. what their words were going to change. what they were embracing as you walked in and they knew you could give them space, security, and a place to rest their childhood.

each time i open the door, i see something new. each time i look into the mirror, i see someone i used to know. each time i inhale a lovely sigh of oxygen, it tickles my heart in a different places. each time i close my eyes, i see the life set out before me. it just so happens to have you there, too.

i do not dance to any religion besides the noise
i hear from laughter around me. my beliefs are
fluid, but i will firmly believe in the universe
and how it gives you the sky above and earth
below. how it blows kisses to a wandering spark
of lightning. how it puts us all to sleep with a
slow and melodic tenure of thirsty thunder.

from the time i was born. my skin never seemed to fit my bones. i could be in two places at once. i could feel three different worlds. i could love and hate myself all at the same time. as i got older, i began to feel real, and not just some idea of what a human looks, sounds, and feels like. i began to see order in my life then a barrage of chaos engulfed what i was and turned me into someone who was never able to be at peace. someone who had to watch over his mother so she wouldn't ambush his little brother. someone who could feel the energy shift and made him conform into a shape in order to fit or blend into where he was. i took on multiple personas, multiple fixations of life just to pass myself for the day. when i broke the bottle, i broke my bones trying to crawl into the pieces to hide from anyone looking for me. there i stayed until i was two plus decades into a lifetime. there i remained until sobriety kissed me, as if it became the mother i never had.

i try not to read everything on instagram or social media. i roll my eyes at teenagers or "young adults" who speak of the hell they only read by Kerouac, Hemingway, or Bukowski. not everything i write is honest, but i have fucking lived long enough to know it always hurts when writing about truth and how some days it is too goddamn hard to do such an act. the next best thing i can do when it hits me, is take its punch, turn it into a fucking feeling, and release it with a gentle kiss back to where it came from.

she lived as if the world was made for her. for those
who could not understand her way of life, they
never noticed how she was the world and the
entire fucking universe. where she goes is not
up to her. nature guides her to new emotions.
the city life isn't what she is after. random
suits her best when love is lost and her
heart is left to heal again.

i love her for all of the reasons my soul does.
she brings both comfort and passion to a
human who forgot how to live,
a man who forgot who he was,
and a soul lost to a war
it never asked for.

i had been scared of my scars for so long, i forgot
how they got there. i forgot what they must feel like
being neglected and not loved for teaching me what
survival looked like when unwritten words appeared
on the broken. to the ones urgently searching
for an answer no man or god can give.

i am after something this world may never give me.
my truth frightens me. i am a child, trying to escape
society who insists on handing out golden tickets to
those who feel as if they have won something for
doing what they were supposed to do. i will continue
running from it all, until i can fucking fly to the
next circus who has more freaks like me. to a
place where my strangeness can hold onto
my hopelessness without feeling guilty.

i tuck my hands into my pockets, look up,
and imagine myself dissolving into something
mystical. i imagine being at peace with the
discovery. i am nothing more than scattered
sunshine in her eyes, but it is the most sightly
place to live. it is where i love her the most.

i once fell in love with a woman who said my name
as if it was something worth protecting. i forgot
everything else because of that moment.

she was never afraid to be herself. she simply wanted
better for her than someone who always made
excuses as to why something did not happen.
her wings are too precious to be handled with
such ignorance and carelessness. her light is how
the darkness learned to love its scars again.

and so we go one. most of us destined for destruction.
the other half destined to find out none of us actually
live forever and realizing they wasted a good portion
of their youth perceiving the end to be some type of
celebration with fireworks, cake, and champagne.

i seek adventure in the form of wandering. in the
purest form of art we have. in the simplest of sighs
and heartbreak. in humanly might and perception.
in the openness beyond the reach of our forceful
grip. the softness is there to be loved,
not be conquered.

lovers do not know how to truly act. i guess that is why
i remain in madly tongues and only reserved for you
to undress me each time we come into eye contact.
your hands have never lied and i fucking adore
that about you.

this life was never meant for me to decide what i thought
i deserved. i have never known anything ever handed to
me that taught me a goddamn thing about life or who
i was. the moon will be hung tonight by humans who
have forgotten what love looks like when it is free.
do not forget to breathe the way you want.
promise me you will remember everything
once it is all over.

when i think of you, i think of all of the love we will make.
i will think of how i get to roll over and have you there to
nestle into, when the sun breaks into our home and steals
you away once again.

i have not had a good cry in quite some time now.
the kind where your skull breaks apart. where your
flesh turns to snow. where your body aches and
pours out demons from your childhood you had
been keeping for a story to tell someone about who
you are. where all you can do is tell someone about
it because you think it will help if someone knows.
where after you are finished, you take your eyes out
to re-calibrate what they have seen. where you go to
sleep and it doesn't feel like you are holding onto
a red balloon, hoping it has enough courage to
take you to the moon to see how she copes with
the energy from all things past and present.
where you pick parts of rotten flesh on
your bones so you can move faster. where you
just fucking let it all out and start again tomorrow.

i will wait for you if you promise me to live your life.
i will wait for you, i will. my life never meant a goddamn
thing until you moved my soul and showed me who the
moon was. until my eyes finally saw you in a full light.

i still do not know if we will make it, but i know my heart
is yours when you are ready. i have already exchanged
souls with you. i know i love you and you love me.
the rest we will figure out together when there
is no space between our naked bones.

only when i love you, do i feel like i can love who i am.
and on the days where we cannot be together, you have
shown me what it takes to do just that. you have shown
me what a broken man can feel like once it is given the
care it had gone without. you gave me words someone
can inscribe on a tombstone one day, instead of just
the beginning and end of me.

i was born into chaos and raised by it for the majority
of my life. without it, i would have never been able to
appreciate the normal side of the universe or the way
love sounds coming from someone who means it.
without fear, sweet child. without ghosts, i live.

whenever i rest, i will need you close to me. my body does not relax until it has your comfort. until then, i will be in and out of sleep, awaiting a dream to keep you here with me. i will always love on your sweet body, darling.
    i will always find ways to keep you centered and dancing under skies of red and orange.

at the end of the day, i am still learning who i am. it is the most beautiful thing about life. we rarely get these chances to sit with ourselves long enough to know how to talk about our pain, our hurt, our love. maybe one day, i can have someone else to tell me about theirs.

when my parents split up, i was eleven, going on twelve.
before then, you could tell something was coming to an
end. i have been chasing after that "something" ever
since, to know how to begin again. it won't let me
sleep and it is what keeps me traveling as much as
i do. maybe i will stumble upon it or maybe it
tracks me down first. i just want to know what
love could fucking be for me.

all of the moments that have happened to me, i keep close. my life, my howl, my unearthly senses, these are the things i fucking feel intensely. i exist because of my willingness to feel every fucking thing and use it to advance my next step, instead of it helping me dig the next grave. wherever it finds me, i no longer feel the urge to suffocate the life out of it.

we do not forget those who come into our lives to love and awaken the mess we at times can be. it takes a rare human to enter that kind of life willingly, only to stay because they found parts of themselves in us. they choose to remain, because leaving means losing everything you had built together. in this life, make your bridges passable. you never know when you will need what is on the other side. if you never end up using it, at least you will have your way out.

i have always wanted it to be you. whether it is now or years from now, my heart will constantly keep your spot open. until then, i will think fondly of your love, touch, and voice, and how all three made me human. everything else around me is just white noise and static acting as life. even the breeze kisses me without passing through me.

my life will never make sense to those who the birds
wouldn't sing for and the sun would never rise and
fall for. the beauty in it all, that is what i am after.
i am after what i was created for, regardless
of the ache birthed inside of me by a universe
still teaching me new ways to survive, while
slowly attempting to love myself.

there will always be something that takes you back to
when you knew what the wild stood for. what it felt like.
what it sounded like. what it made you want to do. i hope
the cosmos returns you there often. i hope it shows
you a new found light standing firmly for who
you are and what you believe in.

we go in search of something that cannot be explained. for us dreamers, we are not looking to define what is before us. we are only here to love, adventure, and chase every glorious star that falls beyond our grasp. a constant quest for the rarest of all moments made by being absolutely free from the world around us and within us. we are here to separate the two and love what is left.

the only thing i know for certain, is that love always comes back to those who have died in its arms a few times. as precious and scarce as it can be, there is only more to find. it is going to bring you back, softly and lightly, one unhinged promise at a time.

there is no need to walk around with the world on your shoulders, when you were born with the universe inside of you. put the mountains down. pick up your breath and allow yourself to sit on the shoulders of the cosmos. it can hold you better than most even on the bad days.

your love will always be important to me. it is the only truth i know. it is the only sound i can feel. it is the only heartbeat that keeps me, me. it is the only thing that can release my soul from this body and take me back to you each and every time i feel lost without you.

there is a stillness around me. if i keep breathing it in,
my bones will forget about breaking. chaos never
sleeps, and neither will my art. demons remain
faceless after the light is gone from a burning
sun. i feel their flames each time a breath is
taken and you are not beside me. my torture
is knowing you are there, but i cannot
talk to you or ask you to hold me.

everything we do is just an abbreviation of who we are destined to become. the periodical standstill we suffer through, makes for long winded stories of our older years, where life meets and greets us with a sun and moon still fucking begging for love to find them.

love is not meant to be babysat by kids looking for a
good time. it is not meant to be kissed gently and
without it being painted on the body like graffiti on
walls of abandoned souls. we keep forgetting how
much we have to bleed for something that is real,
something worth a damn to hold onto until our
fingers turn to letters of every word we anticipate
writing on the canvas of our lovers. love is and
has always been to me, a little destruction,
with an added sense of wild thrown in
for safe measure.

if i can tell you one thing, it is how the light ultimately
finds us all. eventually, your life will become a love
story and survival guide to the lost and hopeless.
it will become the blanket that warms your bones
and the fire that keeps others from being left out in
the cold and forgotten wilderness of this maddening
place. our story does not only save lives, it gives
meaning to those who never feel as if they
have one to tell.

i do not know if i will ever be who you need me to be,
but right now, i am who i am need. it took me over thirty
years to find a sun's light to keep warm by. it took me
over thirty years to find a moon's light to feel freed by.
it took me a lifetime to figure out where you were
all this time i was in search of you. i will never leave
you once these hands get a hold of you.

our souls were meant to be fucking messy, beautiful, and misunderstood. only the crazy know who they really are. oftentimes, others label the normal ones too early. we then wonder why and how we end up living out of our minds, instead of being buried by them.

there may be others walking this earth, but you will always be the only one i ever knew how to fly. i still hope it is you i hold when everything else falls from my body and is buried with the same earth of which we found and made love on. i still have the smile of yours i saved from the last time we talked about life, then began rolling around on the bed like crazed little children. even in the darkness, your love finds me and guides me back to life.

each day blesses me with an attempt to take a deeper breath and learning what it has to say. it is my revolt against who i had been. back when air never tasted like honey or smelled of freshly picked roses. back when blood was a sign of weakness, instead of being progress made. my breath speaks in absolutes now. it is vibrant with age and honesty. may it always find me when my lungs are thirsty.

i am not the way.
i am not the voice.
i am brutally, human.
i am insane beyond
the predication of sense.
i am a conceived hyperbole
made from shattered rock
of a thousand moons. i walk
in the light to kill off any demon
not willing to face me in the darkness.

there is a war inside of me i am finally able to be a part
of. blood, sweat, and soul will be given, but that is what
it takes when the battle comes home and you are alone
with thoughts no longer welcomed. war is what i am
good at. being human is still something that stays
on crutches and is wheeled around, unsure
of the safety rendered when pain is
being left behind.

we are not our pain. we are not who left us. we are not
our shallow graves. we are not what we have been without.
we are what matters most when it comes to staying for the
sake of bringing our scars more light. maybe to live, one
must wander a little more and only love when you are
willing to leave the comfort of your own bones.
please be gentle with me. i, too, fall into water with
a mountain of fear of never coming back up.

all of my prayers are violent attempts of braving the war
brewing in my mind. it is restless and it will not calm
unless i get these words out of me and off my chest
so i can breathe. one can get used to the weight of
continents once you are taking on water from all
of the oceans surrounding you. this castle has no
white flag. this fortress was built on fight,
and goddammit, will i ever.

we are not the scars.
we are the flesh that survived.
we are the flesh of every virgin
star yet to be kissed by its lonely
and unknown goodbye.

violence is only necessary when the soul feels attacked.
until then, if you are to approach me with intentions
unbecoming, you will feel a thousand fucking years
worth of rage. you will see what a wolf can do
when there is nothing left after howling
for a love that never came back.

you have become an easy calm, a peaceful breeze of soberness. my body falls back into a pile of entangled emotions and nothing hurts except how much i love you. it is a beautiful way to live. it is a closing of the eyes and knowing nothing will ever feel like this again.

the way we can open ourselves up to complete strangers is a fruitful way to survive. it is a wild place to find healing. it is a home where windows stay open and everything that once lingered near you leaves without making an ounce of noise as it exits. it is where many find friends, eventual lovers, and everlasting hands that can hold up and hang onto the most tiredest of souls aiming to catch their breath. they just want what is best for you. in this life, it is all we can hope for; a reason to keep going.

i am aged and seasoned. i am a tragically
put together human. i am a slow roast of
a man. i am at times, uncooked and alive
with feelings sprinkled along the veins.
an outpouring of soul is welcomed
and never judged here. i wish this
to always be true.

we venture out into the light, because it is who we are.
there is love to be made there. there are friendships to
be found. there are laughs to be had. there is peace
to be grown. there is you and who you wish to be,
finally seeing each other for the first time.

i am not trying to win you over. i am just trying to know you better and trust myself not to be desperate when talking with you. but if that should ever happen and i go completely over the edge with my feelings, know i have not felt this way since the first time our souls were allowed to speak of being from the same place. back before we were given human names and faces.

part Dylan. part Stones. part Springsteen.
part Bono. part Hendrix. part Mayer.
part Lennon. part Ringo. part Cobain.
part Vedder. part Morrison. part Bell.
part Winehouse. part Joplin. part Charles.
part Waters. part twenty-seven, but alive
enough to know the greats and how they
shaped my life. a part of every age they ever
made it to, but still older than soul itself.
i may never have a best-seller. i will never die
of an overdose, but life is full of magic,
even after they leave or remain until it is
their time. they are the ones you want to
thank and give credit to for who you are and
the influence they had and have on your life.
a page from every book is turned and you can
hear their vocals. their guitar licks. their
showmanship. they breathe differently these
days, but remain full of earthly gratitude from
millions. maybe one day i can have a handful
of reasons that have kept me from burning out
too soon or wandering too far off my own path.
when it comes my time to punch out of here,
i hope there is something more than humans
having a discussion if i was good enough to
live on beyond what keeps us here.

i need to find my way and get back to the place
where solitude isn't my enemy, but my teacher.
i need to relocate my heart and soul, then realign
it with the universe above me. i feel scattered.
more so than ever before. my mind is off in some
distant and desolate realm of imaginational pull.
my heart is stuck in a reality where love is still the
most deadliest game played by angels and devils.
where both are wielding weapons of their choosing.
i look to my left and the angel holds a gun. i look
to my right and the devil holds a rose.

www.ingramcontent.com/pod-product-compliance
Lightning Source LLC
Chambersburg PA
CBHW011141290426
44108CB00023B/2713